SCOTTISH
DRESS AND TARTAN

Stuart Reid

SHIRE PUBLICATIONS

Published in Great Britain in 2013 by Shire Publications Ltd, Midland House, West Way, Botley, Oxford OX2 0PH, United Kingdom.

43-01 21st Street, Suite 220B, Long Island City, NY 11101, USA.

E-mail: shire@shirebooks.co.uk   www.shirebooks.co.uk

A CIP catalogue record for this book is available from the British Library.

Shire Library no. 724.   ISBN-13: 978 0 74781 218 0

Stuart Reid has asserted his right under the Copyright, Designs and Patents Act, 1988, to be identified as the author of this book.

Designed by Tony Truscott Designs, Sussex, UK and typeset in Perpetua and Gill Sans.

Printed in China through Worldprint Ltd.

13 14 15 16 17   10 9 8 7 6 5 4 3 2 1

COVER IMAGE
Four Gentlemen in Highland Dress (1869), by Kenneth Macleay (1802–78).

TITLE PAGE IMAGE
A MacDonald of Glencoe by Robert McIan, wears a plain white jacket, which allows the tartan to stand out very effectively. The historical provenance may be dubious but similar white drill jackets were very popular in Queen Victoria's Highland regiments.

CONTENTS PAGE IMAGE
The style of the uniforms worn by these pipers of the Highland Light Infantry can be seen today on many of the larger pipe bands.

ACKNOWLEDGEMENTS
All images are from the author's collection, except for the image on page 52, which is from Wikipedia Commons, and the cover image, which is courtesy of The Fine Art Society / The Bridgeman Art Library.

Shire Publications is supporting the Woodland Trust, the UK's leading woodland conservation charity, by funding the dedication of trees.

CONTENTS

SCOTLAND'S NATIONAL DRESS

THE KILT and the tartan are not only Scotland's national dress, but unquestionably form the most distinctive and most widely recognised national dress in the world. Strictly speaking the kilt began as a form of Highland dress and is often believed to belong only to that part of Scotland. Yet, while for a time this might arguably have been true, its claim to be the legitimate national dress for all Scots has a very substantial foundation.

Scottish dress shares many cultural similarities with folk dress elsewhere in the world insofar as what was once ordinary working clothing has over the years been formalised and embellished to turn it into a ceremonial dress suitable for high days and holy days. In that respect it is no different from German *lederhosen* or Texan cowboy shirts and blue jeans, for example. In short, it is an outward expression of the wearer's historical and cultural identity and its very distinctiveness encouraged its adoption as a symbol of not just Highland but Scottish identity a surprisingly long time ago.

In popular myth there is something called the Highland Line, identified with the great geological fault slashing diagonally across Scotland from Dumbarton Rock on the River Clyde to Dunottar Castle on the East Coast just below Aberdeen. Those living to the north of this line are held to be the true Highlanders, the original wearers of the kilt and tartans, while those to the south of it are Lowlanders blessed with only the most tenuous entitlement to wear the tartan and none at all to wear the kilt. In reality history is rarely so simple.

Before the Wars of Independence culminating in Robert the Bruce's great victory at Bannockburn in 1314, there is little evidence of such a split. There were rugged parts of Scotland and less rugged parts of Scotland, but neither the English kings who coveted it nor the Scottish kings who defended it ever regarded it as two parallel but different realms.

When King Alexander III tumbled over a cliff in 1286, leaving no obvious heir, the various claimants to the empty throne appealed to Edward I of England for arbitration. Edward duly judged the case honestly in favour of John Balliol, but also took the opportunity to declare himself Scotland's feudal

Opposite: Victorian romanticism personified in all its anachronistic glory, depicted by Robert Mclan in his celebrated *Costumes of the Clans* (1843).

overlord. The Scots were unimpressed and refused to be intimidated, but it took nearly twenty years of bloody warfare to settle the matter. Sadly, for much of that time the English were the least of the Bruce's worries. Before he could lead the Scots army to victory at Bannockburn he first had to fight and win a vicious civil war against the many supporters of the Balliols, chiefly led by the Comyns (or Cummings) in the North and the MacDougalls in the West.

This elegant Highland gentleman of the seventeenth century in another painting by Mclan may look unlikely, but is rather less flamboyantly dressed than a contemporary portrait of Sir Mungo Murray by John Michael Wright.

Their lands, as it happened, stretched in a great arc from Lorne through Lochaber, Moray and Badenoch to the Buchan coast of the North East, and so included most of what would later become considered as the Highlands. Thus the eclipse of the Comyn lords of Lochaber and Badenoch effectively disenfranchised the Highlands in a Scotland thereafter dominated by the Bruces and their Stewart successors.

At the same time the growing commercial importance of the thriving East Coast ports meant that the hinterland (the Highlands) lacking both economic and political clout, steadily became marginalised so that by the seventeenth century there was indeed a Highland line, of sorts. It was always nevertheless a very indeterminate line and it is instructive to note that when the very last Scots Army was raised in 1745 the regiments of the Athole Brigade raised from amongst the Perthshire glens, the Gordons from Strathbogie and Strathdon, and the Farquharsons from Deeside were considered not as Highlanders but as part of the Lowland Division.

It was a similar story with language and if Scots, a tongue in some ways more akin to Flemish and German than to English, became predominant in the east-coast towns, it was still a different matter in the countryside and a form of Gaelic (Buchan Gaelic) was still being spoken alongside Doric in the supposedly lowland North East in the memory of the author's grandparents!

The use of the plaid by the common people was still ubiquitous all over Scotland when the political landscape changed completely in 1707. In that year, by a mixture of blackmail, bribery and outright coercion England, desperate for Scottish soldiers to maintain a bloody and ruinously expensive war against France, forced through an act of Union; henceforth Scotland would be ruled from Westminster rather than Edinburgh. However, although the Scots Parliament reluctantly acquiesced in its own dissolution it was a deeply unpopular move in the country at large. Scotland was now proclaimed to be North Britain and in response its people turned to ostentatiously displaying the tartan as a defiant affirmation of their Scottish identity.

This was most conspicuously seen during the last Jacobite Rising in 1745. When Bonnie Prince Charlie landed in the West Highlands, his first followers were, naturally enough, Highland clansmen, but by the time his army left Edinburgh on the famous march to Derby at least half of them were Lowland Scots. Nevertheless most wore Highland clothes, spelled out in an edict by Lord Lewis Gordon, the rebel commander in the North East of Scotland, requiring recruits to be 'well cloathed, with short cloathes, plaid, new shoes, and three pair of hose.' Other Jacobite officers enthusiastically followed suit and even the cavalry had tartan jackets or at the very least tartan scarves or tartan-mounted shoulder belts.

From a practical point of view this was a sensible enough idea. By dressing everyone, or at least nearly everyone, in tartans and blue bonnets the army was provided with a very distinctive uniform at little trouble or cost. It did not matter that one man wore a red tartan jacket or plaid and the man standing next to him a green one; they were both in tartan and easily distinguished from their red-coated foes. It also did wonders for *esprit de corps* as all of them strutted around

A reasonably convincing interpretation by McIan of a Highland piper wearing a conventional mid-seventeenth-century doublet.

Fine study by McIan of a seventeenth-century Highland chieftain in a belted plaid.

Above:
The Marquess of Argyle depicted on a seventeenth-century playing card. Like the other Scots in the deck, he and his companions are identified as Scots by their bonnets and plaids.

Above right:
Johnstone of Wariston; another playing-card illustration depicting a Lowland gentleman in plaid and blue bonnet.

broadcasting their membership of the Highland Army that had demolished Johnnie Cope's Redcoats before breakfast. Nevertheless, it was more than a matter of simple convenience or of creating the impression that the undernourished children of the Edinburgh slums were ferocious Highland warriors; it was also a political statement.

Prince Charles Edward Stuart was intent on making good his father's claim to the throne of the three kingdoms of Britain, but most of those who followed his banner from choice were equally intent on seeing an end to the Union and on re-asserting Scotland's independence. Not for nothing did some of them carry broadswords bearing the inscription 'Scotland and No Union!' Their choice of Highland dress, whether it was the full fig of belted plaid, broadsword and targe or just a tartan jacket and a rusty bayonet was therefore a conscious display of their Scottish identity. Consequently, after Culloden a thoroughly rattled British government promulgated what is generally referred to as the Disarming Act. There had been other disarming acts before, all of which hoped to ban the use of firearms and edged weapons calculated to disturb the King's peace, but this one was different, for it began by prohibiting the wearing of distinctive 'Highland clothes' and the display of tartan:

Abolition and Proscription of the Highland Dress 19 George II, Chap. 39, Sec. 17, 1746

That from and after the first day of August, One thousand, seven hundred and forty-six, no man or boy within that part of Britain called Scotland, other than such as shall be employed as Officers and Soldiers in His Majesty's Forces, shall, on any pretext whatever, wear or put on the clothes commonly called Highland clothes (that is to say) the Plaid, Philabeg, or little Kilt, Trowse, Shoulder-belts, or any part whatever of what peculiarly belongs to the Highland Garb; and that no tartan or party-coloured plaid or stuff shall be used for Great Coats or upper coats, and if any such person shall presume after the said first day of August, to wear or put on the aforesaid garment or any part of them, every such person so offending …

[f]or the first offence, shall be liable to be imprisoned for 6 months, and on the second offence, to be transported to any of His Majesty's plantations beyond the seas, there to remain for the space of seven years.

The Act was not, as is often claimed, an expression of spite against the Highland clans. In point of fact comparatively few Highlanders had actually joined in the rebellion. Fully as many clansmen had instead marched under King George's banner in the ranks of the famous Argyle Militia or the Highland Independent companies and the other Loyalist militias. The Act of Proscription was intended not to assist in the destruction of the Clan system but rather to bar overt political displays of tartan not as a Jacobite but as a nationalist symbol.

All members of the last Jacobite army wore elements of Scottish dress, as seen in this illustration of a Scotch Hussar with a plaid wrapped around his body.

That the Act should eventually be repealed on 1 July 1782, rather than simply mouldering on the statute book, was a reflection of a growing reassertion in the meantime of a distinct Scottish identity *within* the Union, and a corresponding effort on the part of those Scots who supported it to ensure that it was to be properly recognised as a political marriage between equals; as a true union rather than as a brutal takeover by the senior partner.

The Scots had no qualms about serving in a British army and they were already positioning themselves to play the leading role in the creation of what would become the British Empire, but they were going to do it on their own terms – which included being accepted not as North Britons but as Scots. At the time of the Rising in 1745 there had been just two regular Highland regiments in the British Army: the Black Watch and the short-lived 64th Loudoun's Highlanders. By the end of the century at least a further thirty regular Highland regiments would have been raised and nearly as many fencible or home service units. In fact during this period any regiment raised north of Stirling Castle was almost automatically designated as a Highland one, whether its men spoke Gaelic or Scots or came from Lochaber or Laurencekirk.

And all of them, like Hugh Montgomerie's West Lowland Fencibles from Ayrshire and his Royal Glasgow Regiment, paraded and fought in blue bonnets, kilts or tartan trews to proclaim themselves ostentatiously as *Scottish* regiments.

THE EARLIEST FORMS
OF HIGHLAND DRESS

CLANSMEN are normally depicted wearing the belted plaid, a large expanse of tartan material elaborately pleated around the waist with the surplus material thrown over the shoulder. Then above the waist is a jacket, cut short to accommodate the folds of the plaid and under it a linen shirt; if a more heroic appearance is required the coat can be dispensed with and the short sleeves rolled up to expose brawny arms wielding a broadsword. This familiar picture is, however, completely contradicted by the discovery of two fully clothed bodies, buried in peat bogs as far apart as Quintfall Hill in Caithness, and Arnish Moor near Stornoway in 1920 and 1964 respectively.

The first of these men was actually wearing two complete suits of clothing, one on top of the other. Each comprised an ordinary pair of breeches and a hip-length coat or jacket. He had a bonnet, not knitted but formed from pieces of cloth, and his stockings were likewise pieced up rather than knitted. There was no trace of a shirt although this is most likely due to the linen having completely rotted away. A plaid was also found with this body and coins found in the man's pocket indicate he must have died at some time during the 1690s. But if the style of his clothing and the wearing of ordinary breeches rather than a belted plaid or trews runs counter to what we would expect a Highlander of that time to be wearing, the other body from Arnish Moor turns this expectation completely on its head.

Dating to just a few years later, he was a young man wearing two knee-length woollen shirts, one on top of the other, and a hip-length woollen coat lined with the remains of an older one. There was a blue bonnet upon his head, knitted this time, and a pair of much patched knee-length stockings upon his legs, but he had no breeches and there was no sign of a plaid. This might be puzzling if it were not for the fact that a man dressed in exactly the same fashion, with a jacket and long over-shirt but neither plaid nor breeches, can be seen standing in Inverness market place in one of the sketches illustrating Edward Burt's *Letters from the North of Scotland*, from the 1730s.

In beginning the story of Scottish dress we therefore need to start with the shirt, for that was the main garment described by all the early writers.

Opposite:
A delightful study by McIan of a highland gentleman riding a small pony. Some of the Marquis of Huntly's 'light horse' at Sheriffmuir in 1715 were equally well mounted.

From Quintfall Hill in Caithness came this complete suit of clothes from a man reckoned to have been murdered there in the 1690s.

Magnus Berfaet's Saga tells how when King Magnus of Norway returned from the Western Isles in 1093, he and many of his followers had adopted the costume in use there: they went about bare-legged wearing short tunics and 'upper garments'. Magnus and his men therefore no doubt looked very like some of the Scots sketched on an early charter of Carlisle dating to 1316, just two years after the battle of Bannockburn, but what is interesting there is that while the Scots all wear long over-shirts, it is most unlikely

One of McIan's splendid illustrations labelled as a chieftain of Clan Fergusson but actually based on a print depicting an Irishman wearing a saffron war shirt.

that any of them were Highlanders – which reinforces the point that in those early days there was little if any distinction between Highland and Lowland Scots.

Moving forward two hundred years, however, sufficient differences were emerging for a Berwickshire laird named John Major (or Mair) to describe specifically Highland dress in 1521:

This Scots bowman slain by Sir Andrew Harcla has a hooded shirt and a common style of 'kettle' helmet, so called because it was used both for protection and cooking.

> From the middle of the thigh to the foot they have no covering for the leg, clothing themselves with a mantle instead of an upper garment and a shirt dyed with saffron .... In time of war they cover their whole body with a shirt of mail of iron rings, and fight in that. The common people of the wild Scots rush into battle having their body clothed with a linen garment manifoldly sewed and painted or daubed with pitch, with a covering of deerskin.

Above: One of the earliest known depictions of Scots is a sketch on the Carlisle Charter showing Sir Andrew Harcla beating off an attack by men wearing shirts and mantles.

Right: Highland bowman of the sixteenth century by McIan.

Similarly, Jean de Beaugué, a French soldier who served in Scotland in the 1540s noted, 'They wear no clothes except their dyed shirts and a sort of light woollen rug of several colours', while Lindsay of Pitscottie in 1573 likewise stated that they (Highlanders) 'be cloathed with ane mantle, with ane schirt saffroned after the Irish manner, going barelegged to the knee.' Then Bishop Leslie, writing just five years later in 1578 said much the same, but in rather greater detail:

Another of McIan's paintings of a northern Irish kern wearing a voluminous saffron war shirt.

Their clothing was made for use (being chiefly suited for war) and not for ornament. All, both nobles and common people, wore mantles of one sort (except that the nobles preferred those of several colours). These were worn long and flowing, but capable of being neatly gathered up at pleasure into folds. I am inclined to believe that they were the same as those to which the ancients gave the name of Brachae. Wrapped up in these for their only covering they would sleep comfortably. They had also shaggy rugs, such as the Irish use at the present day [1578], some fitted for a journey, others to be placed on a bed. The rest of their garments consisted of a short woollen jacket, with sleeves open below for the convenience of throwing darts, and a covering for the thighs of the simplest kind, more for decency than for show or defence against cold. They made also of linen very large shirts, with numerous folds and wide sleeves, which flowed abroad loosely to their knees. These, the rich coloured with saffron and others smeared with some grease to preserve them longer clean amongst the toils and exercises of a camp, which they held it of the highest consequence to practice continually.

The way Highland gentlemen proclaimed their superior status by the wearing of bright saffron yellow shirts, or rather over-shirts, did not always produce the happiest of results, as the unfortunate Angus Mackintosh of Mackintosh discovered to his cost in 1592. While he and some of his clansmen are preparing to attack Ruthven Castle in Badenoch, we are told, one of the Earl of Huntly's men

One of Burt's illustrations from the 1720s or 1730s, this time depicting fishermen being carried to their boats – to avoid spending all day at sea with wet feet.

'creeps out under the shelter of some ruins, and levels with his piece at one of the Clan Chattan cloathed in a yellow war coat (which amongst them is the badge of the Chieftaines or heads of Clans) and ... strikes him to the ground.'

Thus fell the Laird of Mackintosh and oddly enough so did the practice of wearing yellow war coats. Nevertheless the sudden disappearance of saffron shirts does not seem to have been a prudent response to the realisation that they made splendid targets, but rather the reflection of a shortage of dyestuffs and fine linen from Ireland as a result of the Elizabethan conquest. It certainly did not result in the disappearance of the over-shirt itself, for apart from the evidence of that murder victim from Arnish Moor and illustrations by Burt and others, the Reverend Mr Ferguson, minister of Mulmearn, recalled that in 1715:

> Those Highlanders who joined the Pretender from the most remote parts of the Highlands, were not dressed in parti-coloured tartans, and had neither plaid nor philabeg, but that their whole dress consisted of what we call a Polonian or closish coat, descending below mid-leg, buttoned from the throat to the belly, and below that, secured for modesty's sake with a lace towards the bottom. That it was of one colour and home made, and that they had no shirt, shoes, stockings nor breeches.

Above: A 'Wild Scotsman' after Lucas de Heere, from the 1570s. The original shows a pinkish brown mantle worn over a yellow shirt with a fine chequered pattern, and blue-grey hose or breeches.

Right: Another Highlander with a claymore, this time depicted by Mclan wearing what is intended to be an early kilt – a garment unlikely to have existed in reality.

It was, in short, a pretty good description of the garment recovered from Arnish Moor. Be that as it may, there is a curious belief amongst some costume historians that with this sudden disappearance of the Irish-style saffron shirt, the mantle described as being worn with it was at once transformed from a nondescript cloak into what we now call the belted plaid. In a sense this is correct, but in a cultural rather than a practical context. Bishop Leslie had already described how the mantle was worn long and flowing, and was at the same time capable of being neatly gathered up into folds 'at pleasure'.

The confusion arises because, as we shall see in the next chapter, the belted plaid eventually evolved into – or rather was replaced by – the kilt. Since the kilt is essentially a skirt-like garment now worn instead of trousers there has perhaps been a natural tendency to also view the plaid from the bottom up, and to see it first and foremost as a kilt or skirt worn between the waist and the knees with an upper part to cover the head and shoulders as well.

Left: The claymore was carried on the back but not drawn from that position. Rather it was unbuckled and unsheathed before going into battle.

Below: One of Koler's Scots, wearing a broad blue bonnet and belted plaid. The weapon by his right side is probably intended to represent a dirk.

17

Yet the key lies in the fact that all of those early observers chose to refer to plaids as 'mantles' and upper garments – robes worn over ordinary clothing either for protection from the cold or as an ostentatious display of their status. In part this was accomplished by showing off the colour and intricacy of their tartans, but it can also be seen most clearly in the early portraits of Highland chieftains. Where peers of the realm might choose to be painted in their robes of scarlet and ermine, and churchmen and scholars in equally sumptuous gowns, Highland chieftains chose colourful tartan plaids in a dazzling display of swank calculated to outdo them all. In those paintings the plaid is often arranged impractically in great flowing folds which deliberately imitate the classical Roman toga but reflect little of its practical origins. And it was not just the Highlanders who did so, for as the tartan assumed a wider political and cultural importance in the aftermath of the Union of 1707, otherwise conventionally dressed Lowland noblemen made a point of draping tartan plaids over their shoulders 'for the credit of Scotland'.

This was no mere 'Highlandism' as would be seen in the next century, for at this time the plaid was worn all over Scotland, from the far north down to the border fells. The fact is that the plaid began not as an alternative to trousers at all, but as the equivalent of a heavy overcoat, worn out of doors in bad weather or on a journey or an expedition.

Above: This Scottish musketeer depicted by Koler is evidently a Lowland Scot, being unbearded and wearing tartan breeches which are too baggy to represent Highland trews.

Right: This Highlander depicted by Mclan wearing tight-fitting trews forms a useful contrast to Koler's musketeer.

Far right: An officer and sergeant of the Black Watch in the 1740s, identified by a sash and halberd respectively.

Appreciation of this simple point also explains of course why there are so many accounts of Highland soldiers throwing off their plaids before marching into battle, at Kilsyth in 1645 for example, or at Killiecrankie. Or for that matter, at Prestonpans in 1745, where Bonnie Prince Charlie was heard to laugh after the battle that his Highlanders had lost their plaids. Yet, given that their everyday dress was a large woollen over-shirt and a short jacket, throwing away their plaids had nothing to do with stripping off their clothing. Instead they were simply doing exactly the same thing all soldiers are wont to do: dropping their packs, blanket rolls and greatcoats and any other encumbrances and impedimenta before going into action.

Nevertheless, once they themselves started to do some proper soldiering the plaid soon proved to be a less-than-ideal garb, as we shall see in the next chapter.

A splendid evocation by McIan of the voluminous nature of the belted plaid, illustrating perfectly why it was discarded at home, at work or on the battlefield.

Highland Visitors – a propaganda piece from 1745 depicting clansmen in plaids being overseen by an officer in trews.

THE 'INVENTION' OF THE KILT

T HE STORY OF THE KILT in the eighteenth century is at once well known, often vehemently disputed, and thoroughly misunderstood.

In March 1785 a letter, apparently written nearly twenty years before by a gentleman of unimpeachable veracity named Evan Baillie of Aberiachan, appeared in the pages of the *Edinburgh Magazine*, asserting:

> About 50 years ago, one Thomas Rawlinson, an Englishman, conducted an iron work carried on in the countries of Glengarie and Lochaber; he had a throng of Highlanders employed in the service, and became very fond of the Highland dress, and wore it in the neatest form; which I can aver as I became personally acquainted with him above 40 years ago. He was a man of genius and quick parts, and thought it no great stretch of the invention to abridge the dress, and make it handy and convenient for his workmen: and accordingly directed the using of the lower part plaited of what it called the *feile* or kilt … and the upper part was set aside; and this piece of dress, so modelled as a diminutive of the former, was in the Gaelic termed *felie-beg* and in our Scots termed little kilt; and it was found so handy and convenient, that, in the shortest space, the use of it became frequent in all the Highland Countries, and in many of our northern Low Countries also.

Needless to say the suggestion that the kilt was invented by an Englishman inspired a great deal of controversy and downright indignation, both at the time and afterwards. However, while the story as it appeared in the *Edinburgh Magazine* is well known, John Sobieski Stuart wrote a slightly different version in his magisterial 1845 *Costume of the Clans*, which he stated was told to him by various old people in the Glengarry country.

An Englishman named Rawlinson was indeed the manager of an ironworks, sited to take advantage of the extensive birch woods near Bridge of Garry, which provided the fuel necessary to feed the furnace. The kilt was devised and sewn for him by a regimental tailor named Parkinson from the nearby garrison of Fort William and when Rawlinson strode forth wearing it,

Opposite: Mclan's rendering of an officer of the Sutherland Fencibles, a home service unit raised in the 1750s.

Above: This
well-known image
of one of the first
Highland soldiers
in the British Army
appeared in
the 1742
Cloathing Book.

Above right:
This sketch after
an unknown
artist from
Penicuik in 1745
might serve as a
rear view of the
preceding figure.

Right: A typical
Highland
gentleman of
the period shortly
before the '45,
depicted by McIan
wearing a 'figured'
(embroidered)
waistcoat, short
coat and
belted plaid.

old Ian MacAlasdair Mhic Raonuill of Glengarry 'caused a second to be made for himself'. There is no mention in this version of the kilt being made for Rawlinson's workmen, who were in any case not foundrymen but woodcutters. More importantly it was at the time being worn by just a few albeit by the rising of 1745 it had become sufficiently popular to be included as the 'Philabeg, or little Kilt' in the Act of Proscription that followed.

As it turned out, the crucial part of that Act was not the mere mention of philabegs but the way in which it exempted those in the service of the Crown from its provisions. Thus began the Highland regiments' custody of the kilt and tartan. Tailors, outfitters and other pundits might express their opinions as to the appropriateness of garments or accoutrements for particular occasions, but ultimately it is those regiments which are the true guardians and arbiters of everything we now recognise as Highland dress – and that includes the kilt. Notwithstanding the impression given in both versions of the story as told above, the kilt is not simply the old belted plaid with the upper part cut away.

We are told that when a Highlander donned his plaid he first laid it out flat on the ground or the floor. A belt was then passed underneath it at what would be his waist level when the bottom edge lay at the tops of his knees. The material was then gathered into pleats at right angles to the belt until both ends of it became visible. At this point the clansman lay down on the pleating, crossing and securing

Far left: In contrast to the well-groomed reconstructions by McIan, this contemporary sketch of MacDonald of Keppoch by the Penicuik artist evidences a much wilder figure.

Left: Similarly this portrait of an unidentified but strong-minded character provides once again a good impression of how the plaid tended to gape at the front.

the belt and material over the front, before standing up and throwing the rest of it over his shoulder, or securing it by a button or a pin by the neck.

With practice this can be done surprisingly quickly and easily. It takes little imagination to work out where the belt should go by reference to the tartan, while the pleating is folded along an easily determined sequence of vertical lines. There are, however, a number of drawbacks not always apparent from formal portraits. Belting the plaid this way is all very well on a floor or a flat piece of dry ground; when it is wet and windy it is easier

Highland clansmen in action in 1745 as sketched by the Penicuik artist. Note again the characteristic 'gape' at the front, of the plaid, barely covered by the sporran.

and a good deal quicker to throw the whole lot over the shoulders and then roughly gather it in around the waist, especially if a heavy over-shirt is being worn underneath anyway.

Even if the plaid is put on properly there are two other problems to contend with. In the first place, because the greater part of it is still above the waist, there is a pronounced tendency for the kilted part to be dragged upwards, thus increasing the gap between the knee and the bottom hem. Secondly, although the material should ideally overlap at the front like the modern kilt, there is instead a tendency for the two sides to drift

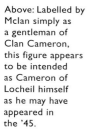

Above: Labelled by McIan simply as a gentleman of Clan Cameron, this figure appears to be intended as Cameron of Locheil himself as he may have appeared in the '45.

apart. Dignity was then preserved by the sporran and the way in which (as some portraits show) the pleats or kilting are carried all the way around, rather than leaving a flat 'apron' at the front. Nevertheless, contemporary illustrations almost invariably depict both a gap at the front and a far greater expanse of naked leg than might be expected in the civilised world.

The result of this is that however useful and comfortable a plaid might have been when worn by an individual, it was thoroughly unsuitable for regular soldiering. At home a man could discard his plaid, either to dry it out in front of a fire or simply lay it aside in warm weather, and then wander around in his shirt tails. Not so in the army. Even when the plaid was worn, achieving a smart and military appearance on parade was possible but required too much care and attention to ensure that each one was pleated, hung and pinned in a smart and soldier-like manner.

Hence the attractions of the kilt were obvious, for it preserved the basic elements of the regimental uniform – King George's red coat above the waist and King George's dark tartan below – but was far quicker to put on and far less cumbersome to wear. In the 1750s Highland orderly books were directing

Opposite, top right: This sketch after the Penicuik artist is a useful reminder that Scottish dress could often be significantly less elegant than sometimes imagined.

This gentleman seems intended as a portrait of the Jacobite general, Lord George Murray. Ironically he wears Murray of Atholl tartan – the Black Watch sett with a red overstripe.

that when a new plaid was issued, the old one was to be cut down and sewn into a kilt, worn on all but the most formal occasions. By the end of the eighteenth century, kilts were no longer being cut from old plaids but made up from new material, which is why in the 1790s the pattern books of William Wilson of Bannockburn, the great tartan weavers, show that the Black Watch had two tartans: the ordinary kilt tartan which featured a red overstripe (of which more later) and the plaid tartan which was of the more familiar Black Watch sett.

Plaiding was woven on a 27-inch width rather than the 54-inch width of broadcloth, and consequently had to be doubled for a plaid. Kilts required just

Right: One of Mclan's prints, this time very closely based on a pre-1745 portrait of James Drummond, Duke of Perth. Being a gentleman, dignity is preserved by his trews.

Below: The classical elegance of Perth's drapery contrasts markedly with the practical reality of this individual identified by the Penicuik artist as MacGregor of Dalnasplutrach.

a single width and this reached up from just above the knees not to the waist but to the bottom of the ribs – where it remained until the arrival of denim jeans in the 1960s abruptly dropped men's waistlines to the top of their hips. This material was then pleated and the top third of each pleat sewn down. The early pleats were still simple folds but once fixed in place it took no great stretch of the imagination to improve their appearance by pressing them flat with a hot iron to create box pleats.

In very simple terms, if laid out flat a kilt comprises three equal-sized portions: a central pleated area, which forms the back of the garment, and two flat aprons which fold one over the other to form the front. When putting on the kilt the right-hand apron is first passed across the body and secured at the left, and the left hand piece is then passed over the top of it and secured on the right.

In the early days it was fastened with long pins and by way of preserving regimental tradition the Black Watch were still securing their kilts with pins at the outbreak of the First World War in 1914. The constant use of pins obviously did the material no good and as early as the 1790s buttons were being substituted, ribbon laces were common, and now straps and buckles are used. Whatever the form of fastening, it is used only at the top of the kilt and never at the bottom, which is unsecured to allow free movement. It is common for a pin to be worn low on the right leg, but this is attached to the outer apron by way of a weight to prevent it flying up, and is not used to secure it as the buckles do at the waist.

In time this simplest of kilts evolved further as the original box pleating gave way in the 1820s to knife pleating – and for some regiments to modern box pleating which is really a variant upon it. This demanded a great deal more skill from the kilt maker for it involved a significant change in the way the kilt was made.

At a distance the pattern of the unaltered government or Black Watch tartan is difficult to distinguish and it appears simply as a black or very dark greenish blue colour. The overstripes added by some regiments do stand

A very useful illustration by McIan of the box pleating used in making eighteenth-century kilts, this time in the Grant tartan.

out, however, and in order to tidy things up at the rear it is necessary to arrange the pleating so that either the same pattern of checks is displayed front and back, or else a closely spaced arrangement of the vertical stripes.

Whichever is preferred, this requires both more material and a fixed number of pleats to achieve the required appearance: twenty-two for the Camerons for example; thirty-one each for the Black Watch, Gordons and Argylls; and thirty-four for the Seaforths. This in turn meant that instead

Right: The kilt was worn by some of the Highland Light Infantry. The pipers had always worn it, as did all ranks of the 6th (City of Glasgow) Battalion.

Far right: The same kilt viewed from the right to show the two buckles used to secure the apron at the waist.

Right: A rear view of the pleating. The Highland Light Infantry regained the kilt after the Second World War, only to lose it again on amalgamation with the Royal Scots Fusiliers.

Far right: The same again from the left, showing the single strap passing through the outer apron to secure the inner flap.

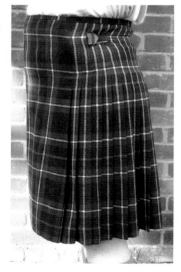

of simply being fitted around the waist with as many or as few pleats might be required by the girth of the wearer, it had to be tailored to fit, with excess material cut away from the top of the pleat. Far from being a matter of casually throwing a piece of cloth around the waist, the kilt was now something that required a craftsman to make it properly.

Above: Bayonet drill as demonstrated in a modern reconstruction: a Black Watch officer from c. 1760 has his bayonet 'charged' towards the enemy.

Front Ranks push your Bayonets 3 times 6 Mo.

Front ranks stand fast as you are, Rear ranks march 3 paces in a line as you stand, center D,? First draw up your left foot to ỷ right heel, count 3 & 2 with ỷ right foot, at ỷ word of command turn your Firelock as lightning over your left Arm, Seizing ỷ Butt & extending ỷ right foot a little further in a line w.th ỷ left, ỷ Rear rank seizing ỷ Cocks, as they turn over ỷ left Arm, keeping their Elbows high to clear ỷ front rank

A Highland soldier demonstrating bayonet drill in Major George Grant's *New Highland Military Discipline* of 1757.

THE VICTORIAN REVIVAL

THE TRANSFORMATION of Highland dress into Scottish dress began with a determination to assert a distinct Scottish identity within the Union. James MacPherson's poem cycle *Ossian*, a mighty epic of Gaelic heroes first published in 1762, exercised an enormous influence little appreciated today. It was MacPherson, rather than Sir Walter Scott, who first turned Highland clansmen into romantic warriors. In the process he also provided a culturally insecure Scotland with a highly distinctive creation myth and a romantic literary heritage firmly rooted not in the douce, respectable Lowlands of John Knox, David Hume and Adam Smith, or even in Scott's beloved wild borderland, but in the infinitely wilder Highlands.

Both MacPherson and Scott would be vigorously condemned by the great historian Thomas Babington Macauley, who wrote of how 'the vulgar imagination was so completely occupied by plaids, targets and claymores that by most Englishmen, Scotchmen and Highlanders were regarded as synonymous words.' In more recent times, other writers such as John Prebble have joined with Macauley in denouncing the 'sweet smell of romantic anaesthesia' associated with the Highland revival. However, easy though it is to criticise the Victorian mania for tartans and everything that went with them, it is also true that it was the Scots themselves who most eagerly embraced this synonymity of tartans with 'Scottishness'.

Respectability came first with a royal visit to Edinburgh by King George IV in 1822. The King himself was persuaded to wear a kilt, and Highland dress suddenly became fashionable.

As ever it was the Highland regiments that led the charge. During the Napoleonic Wars the need to expand their size meant there were insufficient Highland recruits to fill the ranks of all the kilted battalions. Englishmen and Irishmen would have to make up the balance and in order to accommodate them the decision was made in 1809 to take away the kilt from six of the regiments, including the Highland Light Infantry. The move was deeply unpopular, but as soon as the wars ended and the extra battalions were disbanded, those regiments set about regaining their Highland heritage.

Opposite:
With Highland dress being regarded as synonymous with Scottish dress, it was adopted by a number of expatriate Scottish volunteer units. The Liverpool Scottish opted for Forbes tartan.

Right: Ostensibly a portrait of John Gordon of Glenbuchat of the '45, this is a typical Victorian imagining, characterised by the intricate detailing popularised by the Sobieski Stuart brothers (see page 48).

Far right: More romanticism, this time in the form of a print by William Pyne depicting a Highland shepherd, c. 1800.

Right: Kenneth Macleay's triple portrait of Sergeant James Sutherland, Adam Sutherland and Neil Mackay, provides a very clear picture of the major elements of Victorian Scottish dress.

Another romantic view of Highland warriors, heavily influenced by pre-Raphaelism, and depicting the carrying of the corpse of Viscount Dundee from the field of Killiecrankie.

Below left: Grenadiers of the 42nd and 92nd Highlanders by Charles Hamilton Smith in the uniforms worn at Waterloo; note the red overstripe on the Black Watch grenadier's kilt.

Below: Rear view of a soldier from much the same period, in a modern reconstruction. Note the featherless or 'hummel' bonnet and the early box pleating of the kilt.

Opposite, top:
A Victorian
gentleman with
a fine set of
whiskers and
rakishly cocked
Glengarry.

Below: A good
study by Victorian
artist Harry Payne
of a private soldier
of the Highland
Light Infantry.

In 1820 the 91st obtained official sanction for the 'Argyllshire' title, and in 1823 the 72nd did one better, gaining both the title 'Duke of Albany's Own Highlanders' and a suitably striking new uniform to match, combining Highland feathered bonnets with red trews or rather tartan trousers. Next, in April 1834 the 71st were also permitted to replace their plain trousers with Mackenzie tartan trews, and the officers were allowed the Highland scarf or shoulder plaid. The 74th were next, grudgingly designated as Highlanders once again in November 1845 and adopting a virtually identical uniform with so-called Lamont tartan trews.

In due course others followed suit, but then in 1881 something quite extraordinary happened. The government had for some time been working towards a complete re-organisation of the Army with a return to the two-battalion system. This time instead of raising additional battalions the existing ones were to be paired into completely new regiments. Thus the 42nd joined with the 73rd to become the First and Second battalions of the Black Watch; the 71st and the 74th became the Highland Light Infantry; the 72nd and 78th joined together as the Seaforths, the 75th and the 92nd merged as the Gordons, and the 91st and 93rd were transformed into the Argyll and Sutherland Highlanders. Thus amalgamated the new regiments obviously needed a new uniform, and with the exception of the Highland Light Infantry, all of them opted for the kilt. The HLI would have been glad to do the same, but their depot by now was in Lanarkshire and that meant that like the 'Lowland' regiments they were to wear tartan trews instead.

The year 1881 therefore marks the point at which what had once been Highland dress officially became *Scottish* dress, for the Royal Scots, the Royal Scots Fusiliers, the King's Own Scottish Borderers and the Cameronians all adopted tartan trews and Highland-style doublets, and soon acquired blue bonnets and pipe bands as well. So too did the volunteer and later the Territorial regiments associated with them, some of whom were even more enthusiastic about adopting distinctively Scottish uniforms. Two of the Glasgow-based HLI battalions even managed to turn out in kilts, as did one of the Royal Scots battalions from Edinburgh.

The Highland dress so eagerly adopted by these regiments (and indeed by everyone else proudly displaying their Scottish heritage) had evolved somewhat over the previous century and a half, and now it was going to do so again, at the same time becoming more formalised.

Although replaced by the kilt, the plaid itself survived as the *feile* (small), or 'fly', plaid. This was just a small piece of tartan material hanging down from the left shoulder to create the illusion of a belted plaid; during the Napoleonic Wars, officers whose duties required them to wear trousers rather than the kilt adapted it into a so-called Highland scarf. This

Below: The 74th Highlanders lost their kilts in 1808 but nearly forty years later adopted what might be termed a modernised version of Highland dress.

was passed under the right arm, diagonally over the body and crossed over the left shoulder so that both sides dashingly hung down front and back. This is still worn today and is particularly favoured by pipers.

If the kilt and plaid thus preserved much of their original appearance the same could not be said of the bonnet. At first this was a simple round flat cap. Normally it was knitted and felted, although the one recovered from Quintfall Hill had been pieced together from cloth and in 1746 Lord John Drummond was described wearing a blue velvet one. Otherwise the only variation in style is reputed to have been a preference by Highlanders for smaller bonnets than those worn in the Lowlands. What is clear, however, is that although the first Highland regiments wore such bonnets in the 1740s, within a decade they began a dramatic process of change.

By the late 1750s the bonnet was being cocked up to reveal a decorative red band. This is sometimes said to have been a tightening tape but there is no evidence of this and in any case it was soon superseded by a rather broader chequered band. This is sometimes speculated to be a reference to the 'fess chequy' of the old Stuart coat of arms, but its true origin was more prosaic. At this point in time the bonnet was also being blocked up into a relatively high drum shape to present a more imposing and military appearance, and the chequered band was simply a decorative feature pleasingly mirroring the red-and-white checked hose worn below the knee. From its place of manufacture this became known as the Kilmarnock Bonnet.

Then came the feathers. In North America, when the bonnet was still low and flat, Highland soldiers had taken to sprucing it up by adding a tuft of black bearskin above the cockade worn on the left side. As the bonnet grew taller the bearskin tuft was replaced first by a single black ostrich feather and then by a spray of two or three feathers which had the dual advantage of rendering the bonnet far more imposing on parade, while still being light and easy to wear. The problem was that on their own they were too vulnerable to bad weather and bad usage.

Opposite:
Detail from Gibb's magnificent *Thin Red Line*; it depicts the 93rd Highlanders at Balaklava and still forms a major iconic image of the Scottish soldier.

This sergeant and drummer of the Argyll and Sutherland Highlanders appear in a remarkable series of very skilfully hand-tinted photographs of British soldiers in 1900.

At first the solution was to increase the number of feathers until eventually they overwhelmed it to become the dominant feature of what was now a headdress. Consequently, by the 1850s the original bonnet was replaced by an even taller version made of dark blue cloth stretched over a wire frame, still retaining the diced band around the bottom. The crown was rounded rather than flat at the top and once the ostrich feathers were attached to the outside the result was a much shaggier appearance – often mistaken for bearskin.

The feathers themselves were of two types: the relatively small 'flats' which formed the body, and the larger curved 'fox-tails' which hung down

This group of officers belonging to the various Highland regiments dates to the 1860s but shows many features of Scottish dress still worn today.

over the right ear. The Black Watch bonnets sported four of these, while the Seaforths, Camerons and Gordons had five, and the Argylls no fewer than six.

These were worn by all ranks until the First World War, but outside the Army feathered bonnets were and still are only associated with the larger pipe-bands. Everyone else managed perfectly well with more modest affairs. The 'hummel' or humble bonnet – a Kilmarnock stripped of its feathers – gave way to a much neater version, capable of being folded flat and still popular today as the Glengarry. The old flat bonnets remained popular as well and evolved into two styles: the smaller, softer of the two (conforming more closely to the popular image of what a Highland bonnet should look like) became the Balmoral, so named after Queen Victoria's residence; the other, broader and flatter, inherited the name Kilmarnock bonnet and soon after the 1881 amalgamations became the headdress of the Lowland regiments. Both the Balmoral and the Kilmarnock are still traditionally knitted and felted and sport a diced band, but during the First World War were replaced on active service by versions pieced together from plain khaki material. The latter still survives as the ordinary headdress for Scottish soldiers, but by way of distinction is termed a Tam-o-Shanter (TOS).

Highland jackets at first closely followed contemporary fashion except in being cropped shorter to better display the kilt. That soon changed. The Victorian fascination with all things Highland demanded the development of a distinct style of jacket, or rather what was termed a doublet. While possessed of a suitably antique appearance this was both highly distinctive and yet practical. Below the waist there are a total of eight tabs, with two large ones (known for some reason as 'Inverness Flaps') on each side and a gap at the front to accommodate the sporran. The corresponding gap at the rear is filled by the remaining four, overlapping flaps. With the addition of gauntlet cuffs this style of doublet has survived unaltered for over 150 years as a dress jacket in the Army and a favourite with pipe bands.

Nevertheless it was regarded as too elaborate for everyday use. Fortunately in the 1870s the Army came to the rescue once again with the frock jacket. This was just a lightweight version of the tunic then worn by all soldiers, but instead of being square at the front it was cut away in a gentle curve to better display the kilt and accommodate the sporran. Again featuring gauntlet cuffs, this style is still very popular today in tweed or in a colour calculated to set off the chosen tartan of the kilt.

Thus by the end of the Victorian period Highland or Scottish dress had very largely assumed the form in which it appears today, and so too had tartans.

Seventeenth-century Scots bonnets from Speyside (*top*; this may have been worn by a woman), from Arnish Moor near Stornoway (*middle*), and Quintfall Hill (*bottom*).

A fine study of a Highland officer wearing a Glengarry bonnet.

THE TARTAN:
A NATIONAL ICON

TARTANS are a widely recognised part of Scotland's identity but their history and in particular the subject of clan tartans is a complicated one.

All that can be said with any certainty is that after the Union of 1707 tartan was consciously adopted as a Scottish icon and worn by men and women who spoke not a word of Gaelic and might have bristled at any suggestion of 'Highlandness'. Indeed, it is obvious from a study of the paintings of the great portrait artist Alan Ramsay that he had a suit of coat and trews in red and black tartan which could be worn by his sitters, irrespective of family, to proclaim their nationality at a time when walking the streets in those same clothes would lay them open to arrest.

There is no doubt that the chequered patterns which we now call tartan go all the way back to the ancient Celts. One of the earliest references, for example, is by Diodorus Siculus in the first century BC, describing how the Gauls wore 'striped mantles ... covered with numerous small squares of many colours.' Given this Gallic connection it is perhaps fitting that it should sometimes be argued that the term 'tartan' is of French origin and simply refers to a lightweight woollen cloth or *tirtaine* rather than to a patterned material. Certainly in Scottish Gaelic the term *breacan* was more generally used, which can be variously translated but most literally means multi-coloured. On the other hand, as early as 1538 the Lord High Treasurer's accounts make reference to '*Heland tertane to be hoiss*' ('Highland tartan to be hose') and in 1618 an English traveller named John Taylor noted that Highlanders at Braemar were wearing 'a warm stuff of divers colours which they call tartane'.

Be that as it may, the term is now exclusively used to denote a cloth woven in stripes or bands of various widths and colours in a pattern or sett repeated at regular intervals with both the warp and the weft being the same. In other words the same sequence of colours is repeated vertically and horizontally from top to bottom and from side to side.

The complexities of these patterns can vary enormously. In 1581 the scholar George Buchannan simply noted that in the Western Highlands, '... their

Opposite:
In this variation of the Gordon tartan once worn by drummers, red stripes fill between the paired black lines on the blue squares.

Opposite:
Both officers
pictured in this
1900 photograph
belong to the
Highland Light
Infantry.

favourite colours are purple and blue. Their ancestors wore plaids of many colours, and numbers still maintain this custom but the majority now in their dress prefer a dark brown, imitating nearly the leaves of the heather,

The Black Watch
sett is at once
the most iconic
of the Scottish
tartans, the oldest
one in continuous
use and the
progenitor of
many other setts.

that when lying upon the heath in the day they may not be discovered by the appearance of their clothes.'

The choice of colours was most likely dictated by the availability or otherwise of dyestuffs. Just as coats and breeches of hodden grey – actually a sandy brown colour – were commonly seen in Lowland Scotland, most plaids were probably the same. Nevertheless it is unlikely that Buchannan was speaking literally of plain brown garments, but ones relieved by lighter or darker bands and perhaps by occasional brightly coloured stripes.

Another expatriate
unit was the
Capetown
Highlanders of
South Africa,
photographed
about 1900 in
a hybrid uniform
similar to that
of the Argylls,
combined with
the tartan of the
Gordon
Highlanders.

A more useful description was given in 1703 by a man named Martin Martin, who as a native of Skye ought to have known what he was talking about.

The *Plad* wore only by the Men, is made of fine Wool, the Thread as fine as can be made of that kind; it consists of divers Colours, and there is a great deal of ingenuity requir'd in sorting the Colours, so as to be agreeable to the nicest Fancy. For this reason the Women are at great pains, first to give an exact Pattern of the *Plade* upon a piece of Wood, having the number of every thread of the stripe on it .... Every Isle differs from each other in their fancy of making *Plaids*, as to the Stripes in Breadth and Colours. This Humour is as different thro' the main Land of the *Highlands* in so far that they who have seen those Places is able, at the first view of a Man's *Plaid*, to guess the place of his Residence.

The 42nd Kilt pattern as recorded by William Wilson and Sons is surprisingly quite different from the classic Black Watch tartan.

A well-known print of one of the Black Watch mutineers from 1743, displaying once again the characteristic gape of the plaid and the utility of the sporran.

Reliance upon these coloured pieces of wood or pattern sticks no doubt helps explain why certain setts came to be associated with particular islands or localities, just as knitting patterns or smocking patterns are traditional in others. Echoing Martin, it once used to be said that the particular village a Scottish fisherman came from could be identified by he patterns worked into his blue knitted *gansey* or jumper. Similarly, if a particular family or clan was strongly associated with a certain area or a particular island, there would also be a corresponding association with the tartan sett traditionally woven there.

That did not of course amount to the establishment of 'clan tartans' as such, for a Campbell and a MacDonald living on say Eriskay might therefore wear identical plaids. However, one of the earliest hints that tartans had any particular significance beyond the local connections described by Martin, comes from a gentleman named James Philip of Almerieclose. In his account of the Jacobite clans gathered at Dalcomera in 1689, he tells us that MacDonald of Glengarry's men were distinguished by plaids bearing a triple red stripe and that the followers of other chieftains were likewise variously identified by red or yellow stripes.

Almerieclose was a Scot from Arbroath and was therefore perfectly familiar with tartan, so the likeliest interpretation of his description is that as the personal followers of certain chiefs they were wearing otherwise nondescript plaids with a particular coloured overstripe or series of overstripes woven into the pattern, using yarn supplied for the purpose by their chief as a 'household' livery.

A useful parallel to this lies in various Highland regimental tartans. When the first Highland companies were embodied in the 1730s they were uniformly dressed in a dark blue, black and green sett, which survives today as the famous Black Watch tartan. In 1745, however, Lord John Murray became colonel of the regiment and in order to distinguish his men from

Above left:
Campbell of
Cawdor tartan
is the 42nd Kilt
pattern with a blue
line substituted for
one of the red.
This is the
'Hunting' version
in brown and grey.

Above right:
The original
Black Watch
'Music' tartan
was similar to that
of the sergeants
but with scarlet
instead of black.

Above left: The MacKenzie tartan is based on the Black Watch sett but with red and white overstripes.

Above right: This Baillie tartan as originally worn by the Inverness Fencibles is simply the MacKenzie tartan with a yellow rather than a white stripe.

more recent upstarts, such as the Earl of Loudoun's short-lived 64th Highlanders, and the Argyle Militia, he introduced a single red overstripe to the familiar tartan. This survived as the regiment's kilt tartan until the Napoleonic Wars but is now much better known as Murray of Atholl tartan. Similarly, the Duke of Gordon chose the army or Black Watch sett with a single yellow overstripe to be the uniform of his regiment. Ultimately, with the colours toned down it also became the tartan of his clan. The same was true of the MacKenzies who adopted for their clan tartan the army sett with red and white overstripes as worn by both the Highland Light Infantry and the Seaforths since they had originally been raised by MacKenzies.

Whether the district tartans described by Martin allied to the coloured 'livery' overstripes described by Almerieclose and later used to vary the army sett amounted to the establishment of clan tartans before the nineteenth century is highly questionable. What a man wore in his own house was a matter for him and as the old restrictions were lifted there is ample evidence that gentlemen were adopting tartan setts which came to be peculiar to their own family. Just as a good set of tweeds might be handed down from father to son, so too were kilts and other tartan garments; if replacements were required then they would be woven from the same sett.

Just as with Glengarry's men at Dalcomera, the ghillies and other outdoor servants might also be dressed in the same or a very similar tartan, by way of livery. These were often recorded as such in weavers' pattern books, so that this laird or that might conveniently order additional quantities of it from time to time. However, insofar as these were tartans chosen by individuals who were quite at liberty to take a fancy to something else entirely, they were still not 'clan tartans' as such.

The catalyst in fixing those tartans came in 1822 with the visit of King George IV to Edinburgh and the encouragement given to his loyal subjects to turn out in Highland dress and tartans. Because a great many of those intending to do so had never actually worn Highland dress before they soon began enquiring what tartan they should properly wear. By and large what customers asked for they were given. There is a story, possibly apocryphal, that one day the great tartan weavers William Wilson and Sons of Bannockburn received an order from a particularly valued American customer for a very large quantity of Black Watch tartan and as an afterthought they were also asked for a rather smaller quantity of *Brown* Watch tartan! The tale then continues that once the laughter died down the manager solemnly declared that the customer is always right and

Above left:
The red Fraser sett derives from a piece of tartan said to have been worn by a member of Simon Fraser's Highlanders at Quebec in 1759.

Above right:
The McNab tartan displays the same arrangement of checks and stripes which make up the Black Watch sett, but with different colouring.

Above:
The Hunting MacRae can be traced back to the Black Watch sett as it is essentially the Mackenzie tartan with the blue and green transposed.

Above right:
The Cameron of Erracht tartan bears no relationship to the Black Watch sett but was supposedly devised by Erracht's mother, who was a MacDonald.

would somebody kindly give the necessary instructions to the weavers. The story may well be true, for the present author himself wore a Brown Watch tartan kilt for many years, but the point is that if a clan tartan is wanted the customer shall have it – even if it needs to be invented.

Clearly there was a crying need for guidance on this point. Ordering a quantity of say Grant tartan was obviously much more straightforward than deciding between an otherwise anonymous number 23 or an equally anonymous number 30 tartan. Guidance therefore came in the first instance from Logan's *Scottish Gael* of 1831, which included a list of fifty-four clan tartans. It is sobering to note, however, that when Logan sought confirmation of their identity from William Wilsons he was dismayed to learn that many were simply known in the trade as 'fancy' tartans, and far from being genuinely associated with any clan or family most were just identified by number.

Nevertheless Logan was followed by two remarkable brothers calling themselves John and Charles Sobieski Stuart and claiming to be directly descended from Bonnie Prince Charlie himself. Whether they themselves believed this or not, they were genuine scholars and in 1842 published a remarkable book entitled *Vestiarium Scoticum*. This purported to be one of those old manuscripts proverbially found under the bed. In this case it

Another iconic Scottish tartan is what is now called Royal Stuart tartan, although at one time it was named Royal Bruce!

was excitingly claimed to be a sixteenth-century document recording the tartans of the various clans. In reality it was a forgery and soon denounced as such, but together with McIan's splendidly illustrated *Clans of the Scottish Highlands* published in the following year with text by Logan, it firmly established the popular notion that that there was – or at least should be – such a thing as a clan tartan.

The red Grant tartan is itself unconnected with the Black Watch one, although that sett is worn as a Grant hunting tartan.

HIGHLAND DRESS TODAY

TODAY Scottish and Highland dress are very much synonymous. Indeed, it would be pretentious to argue otherwise for since 1707, first tartans and then kilts have been increasingly widely worn as a deliberate affirmation of Scottish identity.

While it may be easy to suppose that a modern Pipe Sergeant striding forth in all the wonderful majesty of tall feather bonnet, doublet, plaid, kilt, great hairy sporran and brilliant white spats bears little resemblance to the humble clansman of yesteryear, that would be to miss the point entirely. Those feather bonnets and white spats might not have been worn at Culloden, but they were certainly worn by the Sutherland Highlanders who formed the Thin Red Line at Balaclava, and before that those same feather bonnets were seen at Waterloo when the Gordons and the Scots Greys charged forward together shouting, 'Scotland For Ever!' This sort of thing surely confers a legitimacy all of its own and so too does the simple fact that all Scots, from the Borders to the Far North and from the Western Isles to the Lothians, have chosen for nigh on three centuries to wear the kilt or some other form of Highland dress as their national dress.

Moreover, Highland dress – or rather Scottish dress as we must call it – is not a fossilised relic of something once worn long ago and ever since preserved in aspic; it now comes in many forms and is instead very much alive, constantly changing and adapting to meet different needs and expectations.

A splendid example of this is provided by Aboyne Dress. Scottish women's dress has not been touched upon so far for the simple reason that there appears to have been very little about it that was distinctive. There is evidence that in the eighteenth century, women sometimes wore bonnets, just like their men-folk. Sadly, if a surviving example with straps or ties and one of Edward Burt's sketches are to be relied on, they did not wear them stylishly cocked on one side, but scrugged down flat, which argues for practicality rather than fashion. Similarly, most dresses and gowns appear to have been cut short or at least hitched up halfway between the feet and the knees, not so as to reveal well-turned ankles, but to keep the hems from dragging in the mud as they went about daily lives that were far removed from the polished floors of the gentry. This, however, was not a peculiarity of Scottish or even Highland dress, but common to all country clothing north and south of the border. Occasionally a fine tartan material might be used to make a Sunday gown, or it might be decorated with tartan ribbons, which were sometimes worn as favours, but otherwise there was nothing remarkable about the form it took except for wearing the plaid as a shawl.

The larger ones were known as Arisaids, which the Skye man, Martin Martin, helpfully described as,

> ... a white plaide, having a few small stripes of black, blew and red; it reached from the neck to the heels, and was tied before on the breast with a buckle of silver, or brass, according to the Quality of the person ... the plad being pleated all round, was tied with a Belt below the Breast; the Belt was of Leather, and several pieces of silver intermixed with the Leather like a Chain.

This description has sometimes been interpreted to mean that the predominantly white material was relieved by fine coloured stripes running in only one direction, but it is far more likely of course that Martin was really talking about tartans with the customary pattern of coloured stripes laid over a white rather than a coloured background. For a time therefore there was a tradition of weaving 'women's' tartans which were identical in pattern to those worn by men except for the white background. In more recent years, however, the distinction

Modern Scottish dress can vary in scope and formality – or the lack of it – but this 1960s family snapped at a wedding is still a typical sight.

51

Aboyne dress was introduced in the 1970s for Highland dancing, combining practicality with a very distinctive Scottish styling.

has largely been set aside and the white tartans are now usually marketed as 'dress tartans' to be worn by either men or women on formal occasions indoors.

Consequently until comparatively recently it was considered sufficient for women to wear a tartan shawl out of doors, or if dancing with a partner to wear a tartan sash or favour. In competitions, for the Highland Fling or for Sword Dancing or any other solo dance requiring something shorter than a ballgown, a curious tradition grew up of wearing men's kilts, jackets and bonnets. However, in the 1970s the dance committee for the Aboyne Highland Games very rightly decided that this was a most unsatisfactory state of affairs. Instead an entirely new costume was devised for competitions, comprising a very full knee-length tartan skirt, a fly plaid, and a tight decorated bodice or waistcoat worn over a white blouse.

This was in all honesty a piece of pure invention, but it was also a very distinctive and unmistakeably Scottish style, and for that reason has proved a very successful one.

The importance and continuing relevance of Highland or Scottish dress can also be seen in the way in which it is worn with varying degrees of formality according to the occasion and the inclination of the wearer. It can be seen in its most colourful and spectacular form when worn by pipe bands and Highland dancers, and scarcely less formally at weddings, dinners, graduations and similar occasions. In the British Army it is only worn by Scottish regiments but Scots serving in both the Royal Navy and the Royal Air Force may wear the kilt as part of their mess kit. Similarly members of the Scout Association may wear it as part of their uniform if they are Scots or are of Scottish descent. It is de rigueur of course for Highland Games and a perfect accompaniment for tweeds, but it is not just for the high days and holy days and can be seen worn with hiking boots and sweaters as well.

And above all, whether Scottish dress takes the form of a kilt, trews, skirt or anything else, the most important and most instantly recognised feature is the tartan.

An often controversial aspect of the story of Scottish dress is the question of clan tartans. As discussed in the previous chapter, most if not all of the principal ones were to all intents and purposes 'invented' early in the nineteenth century. Robertson tartan, for example, first appears in William Wilson's pattern books in 1793. Chisholm and Stewart had been added by 1800, and following the royal visit in 1822 there was a positive flood to meet a burgeoning demand. Ironically although the Sobieski Stuarts' *Vestiarium Scoticum* was quickly recognised to be a forgery, a substantial number of the seventy-five tartans described in it have subsequently been adopted and firmly established as those of the clans concerned. This origin nevertheless does not affect their legitimacy: if a sett needs to be adopted or invented for a particular clan, the fact that it first appeared in the *Vestiarium* rather than anywhere else is quite irrelevant. Indeed it is certainly true to say that having been published as long ago as 1842 the *Vestiarium* tartans now enjoy a fair degree of legitimacy in their own right.

New tartans are still being created every day – sometimes for individuals, families, and regiments, and sometimes for institutions such as universities and even for states. Existing clan tartans are also being adapted in a vibrant and lively fashion not just to create dress tartans, but hunting tartans, ancient tartans and muted tartans, just as a modern football team boasts different strips for different occasions.

Slightly more controversial is the association of seemingly unrelated names with particular clans. These names are sometimes regarded as 'septs' or branches of the clan but not necessarily sharing the name, in order to prove 'entitlement' to wear a particular tartan. A polite enquiry will for example confirm that anyone named Allan, Bissett, Bowie, Buie, Gilroy, MacAllan, Macgilroy, MacKerran, MacKiaran, MacKessock, Pratt, or Suttie can be considered as members of Clan Grant. Similarly those bearing the names Allan, Allanson, Bartholomew, Callendar, Caw, Galbraith, Gruamach, Kinnieson, Lennox, MacAindra, MacAllan, MacCaa, MacCaw, MacCondy, MacEoin, MacGeoch, Macgreusich, Macinstalker, MacIock, MacJames, Mackinlay, MacNair, MacNider, MacRobb, MacWalter, MacWilliam, Miller, Monach, Napier, Parlane, Robb, Stalker, Thomason, Weaver, and Weir may consider themselves connected with Clan MacFarlane.

The plaid as a mantle or outer garment in bad weather.

In Gaelic society a man was rarely referred to as, say, Mr Grant or Mr MacFarlane – if they were all Grants or MacFarlanes in a particular locality it was obviously necessary to distinguish between them. Therefore if a man was possessed of land he was normally referred to by his address; as MacFarlane of Lennox for example, or simply as Lennox. More commonly he might be distinguished as the son of his father and thus Allan or MacAllan.

It will be noted of course that someone named Allan or MacAllan can choose to wear either Grant or MacFarlane tartan according to preference. The reason for this is quite simple, in that such patronymics were never peculiar to one particular clan. Sometimes, however, the associations can be more tenuous. A good example of this is the name Reid, one of the fifty most common surnames in Scotland. This name is held to be a sept or branch of the Clan Robertson, and that those bearing the name are accordingly entitled to wear the Robertson tartan. In reality that association arises simply from the fact that in the eighteenth century a Robertson of Straloch changed his name in order to fulfil the terms of a fortunate legacy, and was thereafter Baron Reid of Straloch. The present author's Reid forebears therefore have no connection whatsoever with Perthshire and Clan Robertson since they have belonged to eastern Aberdeenshire at least as far back as the sixteenth century!

Not that it matters; nothing about clan tartans, save the exclusivity of the Royal Family's private Balmoral tartan, is compulsory. Scots may choose to wear the tartan of 'their' clan, or they may choose to wear something entirely different, 'according to their fancy'. Far from restricting tartan to the chosen 'Celtic' few, these lists are instead a reflection of the degree to which tartan is an *inclusive* Scottish icon, entitled to be worn by all Scots and those of Scottish descent and not just those bearing the names of the great clans. They are in short an encouragement to wear it whether one's name is MacDonald or Smith.

By way of a tailpiece, the curious will no doubt quietly wish to know the answer to the perennial question: what is worn under the kilt?

The answer is assumed to be nothing, but yet while sometimes interpreted literally it is based on a misunderstanding. As we have seen, the plaid was not something the Scots wore instead of trousers, but an outer garment, a cloak or overcoat – and under it they did indeed wear nothing, or rather (usually) they wore no breeches but instead wandered around dressed just in their shirts. This was of course why the slightly scandalised Army put them into kilts in the first place – in order to preserve a proper soldierly appearance. Ironically the wheel eventually turned full-circle: when Highland soldiers in South Africa during the First World War were relaxing, whether during a halton the march or taking part in sports days, they were prone to taking off the heavy kilt and just wandering around in shirt tails and khaki drawers!

An essential accompaniment to Highland or Scottish dress is the sporran, of which this is a typical example. The decorative tassels originated as a simple drawstring fastening.

PLACES TO VISIT

Black Watch Museum, Balhousie Castle, Hay Street, Perth PH1 5HR.
 Telephone: 01738 638152. Website: www.theblackwatch.co.uk
Culloden Moor Battlefield, Culloden, IV2 5EU.
 Telephone: 0844 493 2159. Website: www.nts.org.uk/culloden
The Gordon Highlanders Museum, St Luke's, Viewfield Road, Aberdeen
 AB15 7XH. Telephone: 01224 311200.
 Website: www.gordonhighlanders.com
Highlanders Museum, Fort George, Ardersier, Inverness IV2 7TD.
 Telephone: 0131 310 8701.
 Website: www.thehighlandersmuseum.com
Inverness Museum and Art Gallery, Castle Wynd, Inverness IV2 3EB.
 Telephone: 01463 237114. Website: inverness.highland.museum
Kelvingrove Art Gallery and Museum, Argyle Street, Glasgow G3 8AG.
 Telephone: 0141 276 9599.
 Website: www.glasgowlife.org.uk/museums/
 our-museums/kelvingrove/Pages/home.aspx
National Museum of Scotland, Chambers Street, Edinburgh EH1 1JF.
 Telephone: 0300 123 6789.
 Website: www.nms.ac.uk/our_museums/national_museum.aspx
The Regimental Museum of The Argyll and Sutherland Highlanders, (Princess
 Louise's), The Castle, Stirling FK8 1EH
 Telephone: 01786 475165. Website: www.argylls.co.uk/museum
Scotland's National Museum of Costume, Shambellie House, New Abbey,
 Dumfries DG2 8HQ. Telephone: 0300 123 6789.
 Website: www.nms.ac.uk/our_museums/museum_of_costume.aspx
Scottish National War Museum, Edinburgh Castle, Edinburgh EH1 2NG.
 Telephone: 0300 123 6789.
 Website: www.nms.ac.uk/our_museums/war_museum.aspx
Scottish Register of Tartans, National Records of Scotland, H.M. General
 Register House, 2 Princes Street, Edinburgh EH1 3YY.
 Telephone (0) 131 535 1388. Website: www.tartanregister.gov.uk
West Highland Museum, Cameron Square, Fort William, Scotland PH33 6AJ.
 Telephone: 01397 702169. Website: www.westhighlandmuseum.org.uk

INDEX

Page numbers in italics refer to illustrations